SCHOLASTIC

FAB VOCAB
Greek and Latin Roots

Sheila Wheaton

New York • Toronto • London • Auckland • Sydney
Mexico City • New Delhi • Hong Kong • Buenos Aires

Editor: Maria L. Chang
Cover design by Tannaz Fassihi and Michelle H. Kim
Cover photo © Siri Stafford/Getty Images
Interior design by Michelle H. Kim
Illustrations by Mike Moran

ISBN: 978-1-338-15364-4
Copyright © 2017 by Sheila Wheaton
All rights reserved.
Printed in the U.S.A.
First printing, June 2017.

1 2 3 4 5 6 7 8 9 10   40   25 24 23 22 21 20 19 18 17

TABLE OF CONTENTS

Introduction

Welcome to **Fab Vocab: Greek and Latin Roots!**

Did you know that about 60 percent of modern English words come from the classic Greek and Latin languages? That's why teaching word roots is such an important part of the curriculum. If young readers learn the roots and affixes that are so prevalent in our language, they will become much more observant readers with better vocabularies and comprehension. And that's something that all teachers strive for!

Teachers know how important it is for students to be able to find words within words. Breaking an unfamiliar word apart and looking at its root can help readers get a clue as to the meaning of the word. It can also help writers figure out how to spell multisyllabic words. Studying roots will help students become better at recognizing new words, comprehending what they mean, and spelling challenging words.

The *root* is the base of the word to which we attach beginnings and/or endings. We call the beginnings *prefixes* and the endings *suffixes*. The term *affixes* includes both prefixes and suffixes. Roots and affixes maintain their meanings in most words, so if students learn common roots and affixes, they can quickly learn hundreds of new words. That is time well spent!

> **Sample Words**
> Here are some examples to show how knowledge of word roots can help when decoding a new word. *Tele* means "far off," and *phon* means "sounds." So *telephone* means "sounds from far off." *Bio* means "life," and *graph* means "to write." So a *biography* is a written history of a person's life. *Tri* is a prefix that means "three," and *pod* is a Latin root that means "feet." So a *tripod* is something that rests on three feet.

Suggested Timeline for Teaching Word Roots

When deciding how quickly to introduce roots, and in what order, take into consideration the group of students you have as well as the content of your curriculum (vocabulary words, spelling words, and so on). This book is organized so you can introduce three word roots each week, followed by a few days for review.

What's in This Book

Mini-Posters

On page 8, you will find a mini-poster that lists the Greek and Latin roots featured in this book as well as their meanings. Photocopy and laminate this mini-poster and display it in your classroom as an anchor chart. You might also wish to laminate and display the Greek and Latin roots word lists provided on pages 9–11. Students will find it beneficial to have these mini-posters for quick reference as they read and write.

In addition, each set of three word roots comes with its own reproducible mini-poster that introduces the roots, their meanings, and sample words. Photocopy and laminate these as well and display on your classroom wall.

Growing Words Mat

Use the Growing Words Mat (page 12) to introduce a word root. Distribute copies of the mat to students and invite them to brainstorm words they already know with the target root and add new ones as they learn them. Alternatively, you can laminate copies of the mat (or put them in page protectors) and have students use dry-erase markers so they can reuse the mats. Throughout the learning, encourage students to work with partners to share and write new words on their mats. In addition, students can also use the mat to review what they have learned and check for understanding.

Word Root Tracker

Help students keep track of roots they've learned with the Word Root Tracker. Provide each student with a three-pronged folder, a photocopy of the cover (page 13), and 24 copies of the Tracker page (page 14). Punch holes in the Tracker pages and give them to students to put in their folder. Have students write their name on the cover page and color it, if desired, then glue it to the front of the folder. When you introduce a root, have students fill out the information about that root in their Tracker. Students can use their Trackers to review what they've learned and test each other on word roots and their meanings.

Activity Sheets and Review Games

After each mini-poster introducing three word roots, you'll find reproducible activity sheets that reinforce the roots. A review game follows these activity pages to help solidify what students have learned. After you have gone through all the roots in this book, you will find a final review section with even more games and activity sheets to provide practice and continued support of students' learning. The answers to all the activity sheets are at the end of this book.

Meeting the Standards

The materials in this book are aligned with the following core standards:

- Determine the meaning of the new word formed when a known affix is added to a known word (e.g., *agreeable/disagreeable, comfortable/uncomfortable, care/careless, heat/preheat*).

- Use a known root word as a clue to the meaning of an unknown word with the same root (e.g., *company, companion*).

- Use common, grade-appropriate Greek and Latin affixes and roots as clues to the meaning of a word (e.g., *telegraph, photograph, autograph*).

Mini-Lesson: Introducing Word Roots

Use this mini-lesson to introduce roots to students.

1. Bring in a real carrot with the leaves attached (or bring in a picture) and show it to students. Ask them to name the parts of a plant (e.g., leaves, stem, roots). Tell students that the most important part of this carrot plant is the root because it's the part that we eat. The roots also hold the plant in place and soak up nutrients and water from the soil to help the plant grow.

2. Explain that the root is the base of the plant, the part from which the rest of the plant grows. Say: *In our language, words are like plants. The main part of the word is the* **root***. We can add letters to a root to make the word grow and change. Let me show you what I mean.*

3. Write the word *form* on the board. Say: *Let's think of* form *as a root. What can we add to this word to make it grow and change?* List words on the board as students say them (for example: *forms, formed, forming, formal, reform, perform, transform*). Emphasize that *form* is the root of all these different words they had called out.

4. On the board, write a few more words that have prefixes and suffixes (for example, _graphic, kilometer, microscope, description, conduct_), and challenge students to find the roots. When you talk about each one, reinforce the term _word root_. You might also want to use the terms _prefixes_ and _suffixes_ instead of beginnings and endings so students will start recognizing them as such.

5. Next, provide some practice with word roots. Divide the class into small groups of two or three students. Photocopy and distribute a set of word cards (below) to each group. Students in each group can take turns choosing a card, reading the word, and telling the root of the word. You might even have them write the roots on a piece of paper. When time is up, gather the class together to compare and check answers. Here are the words on the cards with the roots underlined: _project, inspection, erupt, literal, question, uniform, pedal, productive, flexible, certainly_.

6. Tell students that if they encounter a word they don't know, it sometimes helps to cover up the beginning and/or ending to see if they can find a root hiding there. That might give them a clue as to the word's meaning.

7. Show students the Greek and Latin Roots mini-poster (page 8). Explain that many of the words in our language come from the Greek and Latin languages of long ago. Say: _There are a lot more Greek and Latin roots, but these are the most common ones. Learning their meanings and how they work can help you become much better readers and writers._

project	uniform
inspection	pedal
erupt	productive
literal	flexible
question	certainly

Greek Roots

bio – life

chron – time

dem – people

geo – earth

graph – to write

logy – study of

meter – measure

micro – small

phobia – fear

phon – sound

photo – light

tele – far

Latin Roots

duc/duct – to lead, bring

flex/flect – to bend, curve

form – shape

grad/gress – step

ject – to throw

lit – letters

ques/quir – to ask

ped/pod – foot

rupt – to break

scrib/script – to write

spec/spect – to see, look

tain – to hold

Word List

BIO	CHRON	DEM	GEO
antibiotic	chronic	demagogue	geocentric
biodegradable	chronicle	democracy	geochemistry
biography	chronograph	democrat	geode
biohazard	chronological	democratic	geographer
biology	chronology	demographic	geography
biome	chronometer	demography	geologist
biometrics	synchronize	epidemic	geology
bionic			geomagnetic
biorhythm			geometer
biosphere			geometry
			geophysical
			geophysics
			geopolitics
			geothermal

GRAPH	LOGY	METER	MICRO
autograph	audiology	audiometer	microbiology
bibliography	biology	barometer	microcomputer
biography	cardiology	centimeter	microfilm
calligraphy	chronology	diameter	micromanage
digraph	criminology	kilometer	micrometer
graph	microbiology	meter	micron
graphic	mythology	pedometer	microorganism
graphite	psychology	speedometer	microphone
paragraph	technology	thermometer	microscope
phonograph	zoology	voltmeter	microsurgery
photograph			microwave
photographer			
pictograph			
polygraph			
seismograph			
telegraph			

Word List

PHOBIA	PHON	PHOTO	TELE
acrophobia	earphone	photo	telecast
agoraphobia	euphonious	photocopy	telecommunication
arachnophobia	headphone	photoelectric	telecommute
claustrophobia	homophone	photogenic	teleconference
ergophobia	megaphone	photograph	telegram
hydrophobia	microphone	photographer	telegraph
photophobia	phoneme	photography	telemarketing
technophobia	phonics	photometer	telepathy
xenophobia	phonograph	photon	telephone
	saxophone	photophobia	telephoto
	symphony	photosynthesis	telescope
	telephone	telephoto	television
	xylophone		

DUC/DUCT	FLEX/FLECT	FORM	GRAD/GRESS
abduct	deflect	conform	aggression
abduction	flex	form	aggressive
conduct	flexible	formal	biodegradable
conductor	flexor	formation	digress
deduct	inflect	formula	downgrade
deduction	inflection	landform	egress
educate	reflect	malformation	grade
education	reflection	perform	gradual
induce	reflector	performance	graduate
introduce	reflex	performer	graduation
introduction		transform	progress
produce		transformation	progression
product		transformer	regress
productive		uniform	transgression
reduce		uniformity	upgrade
reduction			
seduce			

Word List

JECT	LIT	QUES/QUIR	PED/POD
deject	alliteration	acquire	arthropod
dejection	litany	inquest	backpedal
eject	literacy	inquire	biped
inject	literal	inquiry	centipede
injection	literary	quest	impede
interject	literate	question	millipede
object	literature	questionable	orthopedic
objection	obliterate	questionnaire	pedal
project		request	peddle
projectile		require	pedestal
projector		unquestionable	pedestrian
trajectory			pedicure
			pedometer
			podiatry
			tripod

RUPT	SCRIB/SCRIPT	SPEC/SPECT	TAIN
abrupt	ascribe	aspect	abstain
bankrupt	describe	inspect	attain
corrupt	description	inspection	certain
corruption	inscribe	introspective	certainty
disrupt	inscription	prospect	contain
disruption	manuscript	respect	container
erupt	prescribe	retrospective	maintain
eruption	prescription	specific	maintenance
interrupt	scribble	specimen	obtain
interruption	scribe	spectacle	pertain
rupture	script	spectator	sustain
	scripture	speculate	sustainment
	subscribe	speculation	
	subscription		

Growing Words Mat

GREEK					
bio	chron	dem	geo	graph	logy
meter	micro	phobia	phon	photo	tele

LATIN					
duc/duct	flex/flect	form	grad/gress	ject	lit
ques/quir	ped/pod	rupt	scrib/script	spec/spect	tain

Word Root

_____

New Words

_____	_____
_____	_____
_____	_____
_____	_____
_____	_____

Word Root Tracker

THIS BOOK BELONGS TO

_____

ROOT IS

_____

ROOT MEANS

_____

Reference sentence

_____

_____

○ This root comes from Greek.   ○ This root is new to me.

○ This root comes from Latin.   ○ I already know this root.

Reference words

_____   _____   _____

_____   _____   _____

_____   _____   _____

Greek and Latin Roots

BIO

The root *bio* comes from the Greek language. It means "life."

biology – the study of <u>life</u>; the science that deals with <u>life</u> processes

biography – the written history of a person's <u>life</u>

biodegradable – can be broken down by the actions of <u>living</u> things (microorganisms)

biosphere – the part of the earth that supports <u>life</u>; <u>living</u> organisms together with their environment

CHRON

The root *chron* comes from the Greek language. It means "time."

chronology – the science that deals with measuring <u>time</u> and dating events

chronological – arranged in the order of <u>time</u> that events happened

chronicle – a history or narrative of events that are arranged in the order of the <u>time</u> they happened

DEM

The root *dem* comes from the Greek language. It means "people."

democracy – government by the <u>people</u>

epidemic – affecting many <u>people</u> at the same time

demagogue – a person who appeals to the emotions and prejudices of <u>people</u>, especially in order to gain political power

Name: _____ Date: _____

Life in Words

In each box, write a word that uses the root *bio*. Circle *bio* in each word. Tell what each word means and draw a picture to illustrate it.

_____

_____

_____

_____

Name: _____ Date: _____

Matching Time

Underline the root *chron* in the words below. Read each definition. Draw a line between each *chron* word and its matching definition.

1. synchronize

2. chronometer

3. chronological

4. chronic

5. chronicle

6. anachronism

7. synchronous

a. Something that is out of place because it is set in the wrong time period

b. A narrative of events that are arranged in the order of their occurrence

c. To make two or more things happen at the same time

d. When something happens over and over for a long period of time

e. Occurring at the same time

f. The arrangement of events in order of their occurrence

g. A very accurate timepiece

Now, write a sentence with at least one *chron* word in it.

_____

_____

_____

Name: _____ Date: _____

For the People

What does the root *dem* mean?

_____

Fill in the blanks with the correct *dem* words from the box.

democracy	demographics	epidemic
demagogue	democratic	

1. The _____ caused lots of people to get sick in the city.

2. The United States has this kind of government: _____.

3. If we wanted to learn more about the people who go to our school,

   we would look at the _____.

4. The two main political parties of the United States are the Republican and

   _____ parties.

5. A leader who gains popularity by stirring up
   the emotions and prejudices of people

   is called a _____.

Looking for Roots

Number of Players: 2

Materials
- Looking for Roots game board, one for each player (page 21)
- 5 special objects to find (wrapped candy pieces are fun to use)
- About 30 counters (for example, buttons, rocks, pennies)
- A folder or something to use as a screen between the players

How to Play

1. Players sit on opposite sides with a divider between them so they cannot see each other's board.

2. One player places the five objects on any five words on his board. The other player then tries to find the objects by asking about different words; for example, "Is something on *democracy*?"

3. If there is no object there, the asking player places one of her counters on that word on her game board so she'll know that she's already asked about it. If there is an object, the asking player can take the object and place it on her own board. But first she has to name the root.

4. When all of the objects have been found, players switch roles and play again.

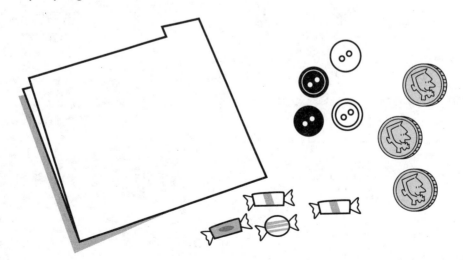

Looking for Roots

biology	chronology	democracy	antibiotic
chronicle	democrat	bionic	synchronize
demographic	biosphere	epidemic	biometrics
chronometer	biome	demography	biohazard
democratic	biodegradable	biography	chronological
chronic	demagogue	chronically	biochemistry
democratize	biodiversity	biorhythm	chronograph

GEO

The root *geo* comes from the Greek language. It means "earth."

geography – the science that deals with the natural features of the <u>earth</u>

geology – the science that deals with the history of the <u>earth</u>, especially by studying rocks

geothermal – having to do with the heat of the <u>earth's</u> interior

GRAPH

The root *graph* comes from the Greek language. It means "to write."

biography – the <u>written</u> history of a person's life

autograph – a person's signature <u>written</u> by hand

graphite – a soft black form of carbon used in lead pencils to <u>write</u> with

LOGY

The root *logy* comes from the Greek language. It means "study of."

biology – the <u>study of</u> life; the science that deals with life processes

chronology – the <u>study of</u> measuring time and dating events

zoology – the <u>study of</u> animals and their classifications

Name: _____   Date: _____

A World of Words

How many words can you make with the root *geo*? List them below.

_____	_____
_____	_____
_____	_____
_____	_____
_____	_____
_____	_____
_____	_____

Now, write a sentence with at least one *geo* word in it.

_____

_____

_____

Fab Vocab: Greek and Latin Roots **23**

Name: _____   Date: _____

Write On!

Write the root *graph* or *graphy* after each prefix in the box below. Then read each sentence and fill in the blank with the correct word. One of the answers will not need a prefix.

bio	photo	tele	auto
para	poly	seismo	calli

1. He used a camera to take a _____.

2. The singer signed his _____ on his picture.

3. The policeman used a _____ on the witness to see if he was telling the truth.

4. She used fancy writing called _____ on the dinner invitations.

5. The _____ recorded how strong the earthquake was.

6. The teacher told the students to write a _____ about the book they read.

7. Before there were telephones, messages were sent from town to town by _____.

8. During math we made a bar _____.

Put the prefix you didn't use with *graphy* to make a new word. On the back of this page, write a sentence using that word to show its meaning.

Name: _____ Date: _____

Let's Study

Read the words. Underline all of the letters except for the root, then write what each word is the study of.

1. mythology   the study of _____

2. ecology   the study of _____

3. biology   the study of _____

4. zoology   the study of _____

5. chronology   the study of _____

6. musicology   the study of _____

7. audiology   the study of _____

8. geology   the study of _____

9. criminology   the study of _____

Can you think of more words with *logy* as the root? Write them below.

_____

_____

Word Root Capture

Number of Players: 2

Materials
- Word Root Capture game board* (page 27)
- Word Root Capture recording sheet, for each player (page 28)
- Wipe-off marker, pens, or pencils

  *You can laminate the game board or put it in a sheet protector for students to use with wipe-off markers. Alternatively, you can make photocopies of the game board.

How to Play
1. The object of this game is to capture as many words as possible.

2. Players take turns drawing a line from one dot to another dot right next to it (horizontally or vertically only).

3. If a player is able to draw a line that completes a box, she captures that space and puts her initial in it. Whenever a player completes a box, he or she gets another turn.

4. If a word is in the "captured" space, the player reads aloud the word and both players write the word on their recording sheets in the correct column. After all words have been captured, players wipe off their game board to play another round.

Teacher: You may want to circulate around the room to listen to students read their words.

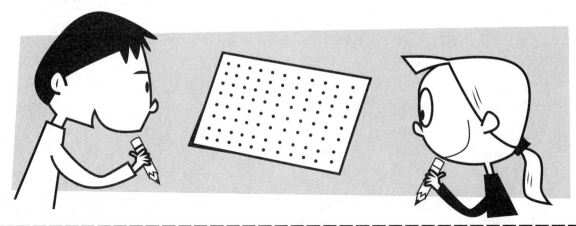

Word Root Capture

mythology

seismograph

geometer

geocentric

graphite

pictograph

geomagnetic

graph

geology

technology

biology

audiology

polygraph

geometry

geographer

criminology

telegraph

autograph

geode

zoology

photograph

paragraph

graphic

geophysical

geothermal

geologist

psychology

phonograph

Name: _____ Date: _____

Word Root Capture: Recording Sheet

geo	graph	logy

METER

The root *meter* comes from the Greek language. It means "measure."

meter – a <u>measuring</u> tool

speedometer – an instrument that <u>measures</u> speed

thermometer – an instrument that <u>measures</u> temperature

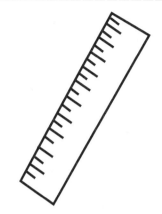

MICRO

The root *micro* comes from the Greek language. It means "small."

microscope – an instrument for viewing magnified images of <u>small</u> objects

microorganism – an organism too <u>small</u> to be seen with unaided eyes

micron – one millionth of a meter (which is very <u>small</u>!)

PHOBIA

The root *phobia* comes from the Greek language. It means "fear."

claustrophobia – the <u>fear</u> of being in closed or narrow spaces

arachnophobia – an abnormal <u>fear</u> of spiders

agoraphobia – the <u>fear</u> of crowds, public places, or open areas

Name: _____ Date: _____

Measure This!

What does the root *meter* mean?

_____

Read the *meter* words in the box below. Use them to answer the questions.

diameter	meter	speedometer	audiometer
centimeter	pedometer	barometer	kilometer

1. What would you use to measure
   how well someone hears?   _____

2. What would a walker use
   to measure how many steps he takes?   _____

3. What would you use to
   measure long distances?   _____

4. What would a meteorologist
   use to measure atmospheric pressure?   _____

5. What would you use to measure
   how fast a car is going?   _____

6. What would you use to measure
   the length of a pencil?   _____

7. What do you call the
   measurement of how wide a circle is?   _____

8. What would you use to measure
   the length of a classroom?   _____

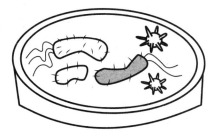
Name: _____ Date: _____

Small Stuff

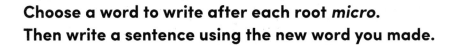

Choose a word to write after each root _micro_.
Then write a sentence using the new word you made.

surgery	wave	phone	scope
organism	manage	computer	biology

1. micro_____ _____

_____

_____

2. micro_____ _____

_____

_____

3. micro_____ _____

_____

_____

4. micro_____ _____

_____

_____

5. micro_____ _____

_____

_____

6. micro_____ _____

_____

_____

Name: _____ Date: _____

Fear Not!

Underline the root in the words below. Then read each puzzle clue. Find the right *phobia* word in the box and write it in the puzzle.

| arachnophobia | phobia | ergophobia | hydrophobia |
| acrophobia | agoraphobia | claustrophobia | |

Across

 1. Fear
 5. Fear of crowds
 6. Fear of being in closed spaces

Down

 2. Fear of water
 3. Fear of work
 4. Fear of spiders
 5. Fear of heights

© Sheila Wheaton, Scholastic Inc.

Acropolis

Number of Players: 4

Materials
- Acropolis game board* (pages 34–35)
- Set of 20 Acropolis cards** (page 36)
  *Photocopy the pages and glue them on the inside of a file folder.
  **Photocopy the cards onto cardstock so words will not show through.

How to Play

1. Shuffle the cards and arrange them facedown in rows in the middle of the game board.

2. The first player picks a card, reads aloud the word on it, and checks to see if the word is on his side of the board. If it is, the player puts the card on its space with the word facing up. If not, the player puts the card back facedown on the board. The next player takes a turn.

3. Play continues until all players have filled their sides of the board.

4. To start a new round, shuffle the cards and place them facedown on the game board again. Each player takes a different side of the board.

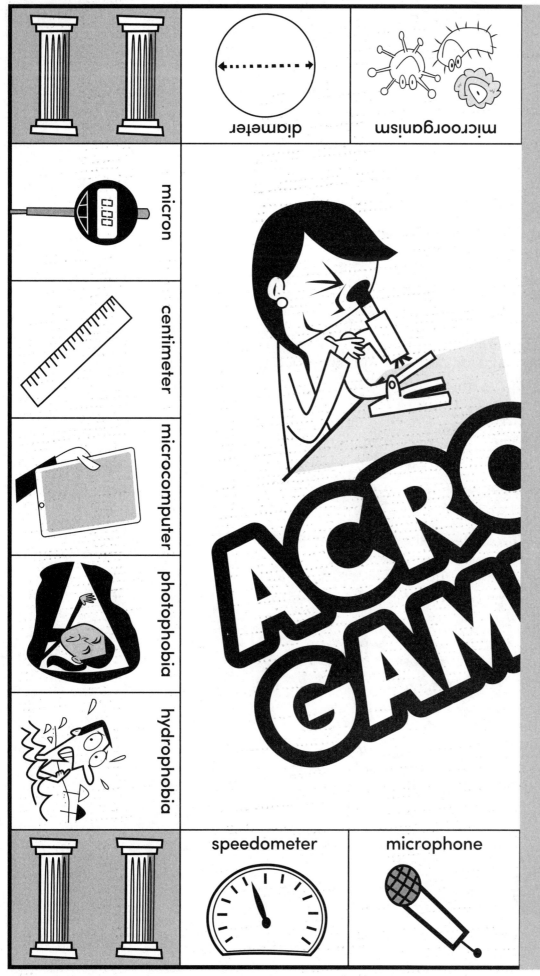

diameter

microorganism

micron

centimeter

microcomputer

photophobia

hydrophobia

speedometer

microphone

thermometer

phobia

microscope

barometer

acrophobia

microwave

meter

claustrophobia

arachnophobia

kilometer

6.5 km

95 km

micromanage

Acropolis Word Cards

microscope	hydrophobia	photophobia	phobia	meter
arachnophobia	micron	diameter	kilometer	microwave
thermometer	centimeter	speedometer	micromanage	acrophobia
microorganism	microcomputer	microphone	claustrophobia	barometer

PHON

The root *phon* comes from the Greek language. It means "sound."

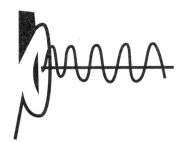

telephone – an instrument for sending and receiving <u>sound</u> over a long distance

microphone – an instrument that converts sound waves into electrical currents to transmit or record <u>sound</u>

phonics – relating to or producing <u>sounds</u> of speech

PHOTO

The root *photo* comes from the Greek language. It means "light."

photography – a process of producing images on a sensitive surface (like film) by the action of <u>light</u>

photosynthesis – the process by which plants make their food from carbon dioxide, water, and sun<u>light</u>

photometer – an instrument for measuring the intensity of <u>light</u>

TELE

The root *tele* comes from the Greek language. It means "far."

telephone – an instrument for sending and receiving sound over <u>far</u> distances

telescope – an instrument for viewing objects that are <u>far</u> away

telephoto – a type of camera lens that makes an object that is <u>far</u> away look bigger and closer

Name: _____   Date: _____

Sound Out

Write the root *phon* next to each prefix or suffix in the box. Then read each sentence and fill in the blank with the correct word. (Note: If *phon* is at the end of the word, you will need to add the letter *e* to make *phone*.)

micro	ear	head	mega
xylo	tele	saxo	ics

1. The cheerleader used a _____ to shout out the cheers.

2. She put on the _____ so that no one around her would hear the music she was listening to.

3. I use my mouth and fingers to play music on my _____.

4. My teacher used _____ to teach me about the sounds that letters make in words.

5. Alexander Graham Bell invented the _____ in 1876.

6. It was hard to hear the speaker in the big room because his _____ didn't work.

7. He used little wooden hammers to play the _____.

8. The reporter put an _____ in his ear so that the director could talk to him during the newscast.

Underline the root word in *symphony*. Then, on the back of this page, write a sentence using the word.

Name: _____ Date: _____

Spotlight on Words

Choose five words that contain the root *photo* and that you don't know very well. Look up each word in a dictionary and write its definition. Then write a sentence for reference.

WORD	DEFINITION	REFERENCE SENTENCE

Name: _____   Date: _____

Go the Distance

Choose a suffix from below to write after each root *tele*.
Then write a sentence using the new word you made.

cast	graph	phone	scope
pathy	vision	photo	commute

1. tele_____   _____

_____

2. tele_____   _____

_____

3. tele_____   _____

_____

4. tele_____   _____

_____

5. tele_____   _____

_____

6. tele_____   _____

_____

Word Root Connect

Number of Players: 2

Materials
- Word Root Connect game board (page 42)
- At least 28 markers for each player (a different kind for each player, such as pennies [heads/tails] or two colors of beads or buttons)

How to Play

1. Players sit side by side in front of the game board so they can both read the words.

2. Players take turns putting one of their markers on a space and reading the word. The goal is to get four markers in a row (horizontally, vertically, or diagonally).

3. The round is over when one of the players has four words in a row.

4. Continue playing rounds, alternating who takes the first turn. Older students may want to be challenged with connecting five or even six words in a row.

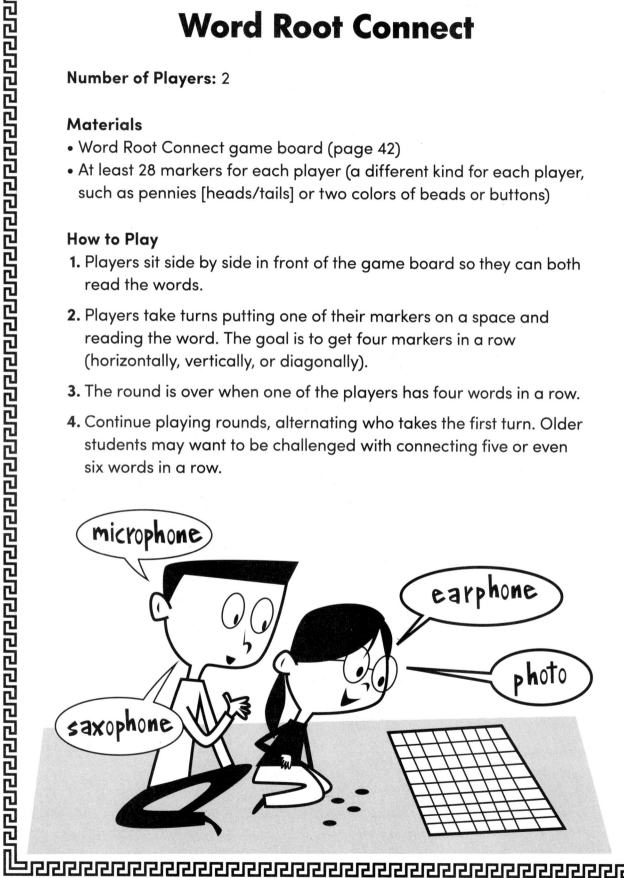

Word Root Connect

phon, photo, tele

photosynthesis	phoneme	telephone	phonics	photometer	telegraph	symphony
photo	microphone	television	phonograph	telescope	telephoto	saxophone
telecast	megaphone	photocopy	telegram	xylophone	photon	headphone
telepathy	earphone	photophobia	telecommute	telecourse	photographer	photometer
photography	symphony	telegraph	photometer	phonics	telephone	phoneme
photogenic	saxophone	telescope	photon	phonograph	television	microphone
photoelectric	headphone	telephoto	xylophone	telegram	photocopy	megaphone
telethon	photometer	photographer	telecourse	telecommute	photophobia	earphone

Fab Vocab: Greek and Latin Roots

DUC/DUCT

The roots *duc* and *duct* come from Latin. They mean "to lead or bring forward."

conduct – to <u>lead</u>, guide, or escort

produce – to <u>bring</u> about or make, especially in manufacturing

introduce – to <u>lead</u> or <u>bring</u> in for the first time

FLEX/FLECT

The roots *flex* and *flect* come from Latin. They mean "to bend or curve."

flexible – capable of being <u>bent</u> or changed

reflect – to <u>bend</u> or cast back, like with light, heat, and sound

reflex – an automatic response; <u>bent</u> or directed back

FORM

The root *form* comes from Latin. It means "shape."

landform – the <u>shape</u> of the land's surface

transform – to change in <u>shape</u>, structure, appearance, or character

uniform – of the same <u>shape</u> or structure

Name: _____ Date: _____

Follow Our Lead

Underline the root in the words below.
Then find the words in the word search.
Words can run across, down, or diagonally.

induce	product	introduction	produce	conductor
abduct	reduce	deduct	productive	education

```
V  I  L  T  E  D  U  C  A  T  I  O  N  Q
C  B  Q  U  R  E  D  U  C  E  E  P  O  N
P  O  T  O  G  H  I  H  T  U  E  P  O  A
R  I  N  D  U  C  E  K  C  C  X  I  G  F
O  G  N  D  P  R  O  D  U  C  T  I  V  E
D  H  Q  U  U  H  T  D  S  C  V  M  X  Z
U  O  A  B  G  C  O  O  U  S  P  E  S  B
C  T  P  S  U  R  T  D  B  X  L  O  M  N
T  X  O  D  P  U  O  O  E  E  I  A  Y  V
W  X  B  C  C  R  D  Q  R  D  Z  U  C  S
U  A  S  X  T  V  S  O  R  X  U  Y  H  W
Y  Z  O  N  D  X  I  O  D  J  O  C  X  X
V  G  I  M  D  X  T  I  O  X  Y  C  T  Z
S  C  F  K  S  W  S  G  W  T  B  B  A  D
```

Name: _____   Date: _____

Around the Bend

Underline the root *flex* or *flect* in the words below. Then read each sentence and fill in the blank with the correct word.

reflector	deflect	flex
reflection	reflex	flexible

1. The baby smiled at his _____ in the mirror.

2. When we have a substitute teacher, we have to be _____ because our routine is different.

3. The goalie used his hands to _____ the soccer ball coming his way.

4. The strong man liked to show off and _____ his muscles.

5. The doctor taps my knee to see how good my _____ is.

6. He has a _____ on the back of his bike so drivers can see him at night.

Name: _____   Date: _____

Any Shape or Form

What does the root *form* mean? _____

How many words can you make with *form* as the root? Write them below.

_____	_____
_____	_____
_____	_____
_____	_____
_____	_____
_____	_____
_____	_____

Now write a sentence with at least one *form* word in it.

_____

_____

Root Reflex

Number of Players: 2

Materials
- Set of Root Reflex cards* (page 48–49)
- Paper or wipe-off board

*Photocopy the cards on cardstock so words will not show through.

How to Play
1. Players should decide which word root they will look for: *duc, duct, flex, flect,* or *form.* Write the root on a piece of paper or wipe-off board so both players can see.

2. Shuffle the cards. Divide the cards into two equal piles, one for each player, with the words facing down.

3. Players take turns saying, "Go." At the same time, each player turns over the top card from his or her pile.

4. The first player to see and say the root they are looking for gets to keep the card. For example, if the target root is *flex* and one of the cards says *flexible,* the player says, "Flex!"

5. Whoever says the word root first gets a chance to read the word on the card. If the player reads the word correctly, he gets to keep the card. If he can't read the word, the other player gets to try and possibly keep the card. If neither one can read the word, players can put the card aside so they can ask a classmate or teacher to help them read the word before the next round of play.

6. If a player says, "Flex," and there is no *flex* word, she has to give the other player one of the cards she has won. If there are two correct words and both players say, "Flex," they each get to read and keep a card, regardless of who says it first.

7. When all of the cards have been played, shuffle them again and choose a new root for another round. (Note: Some of the words on the cards don't have **any** roots!)

conduct	induce	flexible	deflect
educate	product	reflex	inflection
introduce	reduce	reflector	formation
deduct	abduct	reflection	uniform

duc/duct, flex/flect, form

Root Reflex Cards

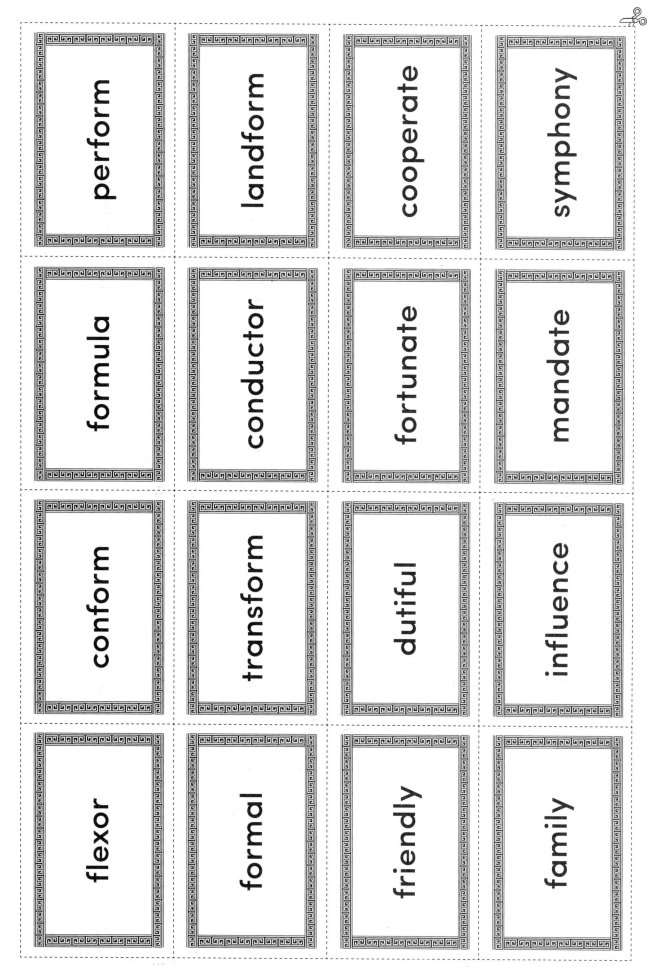

perform	landform	cooperate	symphony
formula	conductor	fortunate	mandate
conform	transform	dutiful	influence
flexor	formal	friendly	family

GRAD/GRESS

The roots *grad* and *gress* come from Latin. They mean "step."

grade – position in a scale, or <u>steps</u> of rank, quality, or order; a mark to show accomplishment in school

gradual – proceeding or changing by <u>steps</u> or degrees

progress – a forward movement by <u>steps</u> or degrees

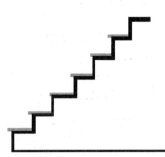

JECT

The root *ject* comes from Latin. It means "to throw."

project – to <u>throw</u> something forward (could be an object, image, beam of light)

eject – to drive or <u>throw</u> out

interject – to <u>throw</u> in between or among other things

LIT

The root *lit* comes from Latin. It means "letters."

literate – able to read and write <u>letters</u>

literature – written works (using <u>letters</u>) that deal with ideas of interest

alliteration – the repetition of initial sounds (made by <u>letters</u>) in adjacent words or syllables

Name: _____ Date: _____

Watch Your Step!

**Underline the root *grad* or *gress* in the words below. Read each definition.
Draw a line between each *grad* or *gress* word and its matching definition.**

1. aggressive

2. grade

3. regress

4. progress

5. biodegradable

6. gradual

7. digress

8. graduation

a. A mark to show accomplishment in school

b. Can be broken down by microorganisms

c. Changing or happening slowly, step by step

d. Showing hostile or destructive behavior

e. The act of finishing a course of study

f. To wander away from the topic in writing or speaking

g. The forward movement by step

h. To go back to a lower level

Now write a sentence with at least one *grad* or *gress* word in it.

_____

_____

_____

Name: _____   Date: _____

Throw Some Words Around

Underline the root in the words below. Then read each puzzle clue.
Find the right *ject* word in the box and write it in the puzzle.

project	interject	projectile	dejection
inject	object	trajectory	eject

Across

2. To throw out
6. Depression
7. To protest or oppose something
8. To throw in between or among things

Down

1. To throw forward
3. The curve of an object in space
4. To force into something, like using a needle and syringe to push medicine into a body
5. A thing that is thrown by an external force

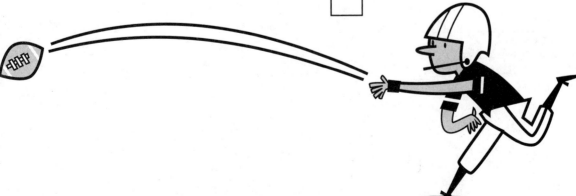

Name: _____ Date: _____

To the Letter

Choose five words that contain the root *lit* and that you don't know very well. Look up each word in a dictionary, and write its definition. Then write a sentence for reference.

WORD	DEFINITION	REFERENCE SENTENCE

Word Root Dominoes

Number of Players: 2

Materials
- Word Root Dominoes (pages 55–56)
- Small brown paper bag to put the dominoes in

How to Play

1. Mix up the dominoes and put them in the paper bag. (If you photocopy the dominoes on cardstock, you can also stack them facedown to one side.)

2. Each player draws five dominoes and places them in front of him or her. A player draws one more domino and puts it in the middle to begin the game.

3. The next player looks at her dominoes. If she has a word that matches the root—*grad, gress, ject,* or *lit*—of one of the words on the beginning domino, she reads the matching words and says, for example, "*Graduate* and *grade* have the root *grad.*" The player then places her domino next to the beginning domino, either end-to-end or to the side.

4. If the player doesn't have a matching word, she must draw dominoes from the bag until she can put one down at either end of the domino path. Likewise, if a player runs out of dominoes, he draws one from the bag until he can make a match.

5. Players continue taking turns in this way until all of the dominoes are used or no more can be played. Players can mix up the dominoes and play again.

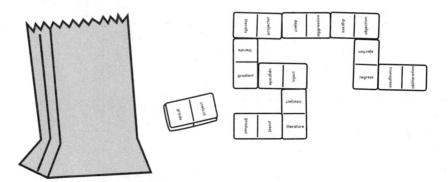

Word Root Dominoes

grade	project
literal	gradual
projectile	graduate

interject	literature
progress	trajectory
progression	object

literary	egress
objection	digress
alliteration	eject

regress	ejection
obliterate	aggressive
deject	aggression

Word Root Dominoes

dejection — degradable	litany — downgrade	literate — gradient
inject — upgrade	injections — illiterate	digression — literacy
regression — illiteracy	projection — alliterative	projector — literally
interjection — graduation	trajectory — centigrade	obliteration — transgress

QUES/QUIR

The roots *ques* and *quir* come from Latin.
They mean "to ask."

inquire – to investigate, examine, or <u>ask</u> questions

question – to interrogate, quiz, inquire, or <u>ask</u>

request – to <u>ask</u> for something

PED/POD

The roots *ped* and *pod* come from Latin.
They mean "foot."

pedal – a lever worked by the <u>foot</u>

pedestrian – a walker going on <u>foot</u>

tripod – something that rests on three legs (or <u>feet</u>)

RUPT

The root *rupt* comes from Latin.
It means "to break."

erupt – to <u>break</u> through a surface

rupture – a <u>breaking</u> or tearing apart

interrupt – to <u>break</u> off or stop in the middle of something

Name: _____   Date: _____

Word Quest

Underline the root in the words below. Then find the words in the word search. Words can run across, down, or diagonally.

inquire	inquiry	request	question
questionable	quest	questionnaire	inquest

```
V  Q  D  B  R  D  C  I  N  Q  U  I  R  E
K  J  Z  Z  H  G  L  K  T  F  Q  S  W  A
Q  T  Z  R  M  Q  Q  Z  K  R  W  L  P  E
Z  Q  X  E  M  M  M  A  O  L  Y  C  L  L
Z  I  N  Q  U  E  S  T  G  I  G  B  G  N
I  E  N  U  P  U  K  I  H  C  A  F  O  K
N  Q  U  E  S  T  I  O  N  N  A  I  R  E
Q  L  T  S  D  W  B  G  O  E  T  H  T  I
U  Z  Q  T  Q  R  Z  I  Z  S  J  S  F  N
I  T  A  X  I  N  T  J  E  T  I  K  T  M
R  F  J  S  P  S  O  U  S  E  S  S  H  Q
Y  U  W  R  E  B  Q  E  D  O  T  H  N  B
C  X  P  U  R  V  U  L  O  X  A  B  C  A
X  N  Q  O  Z  Q  G  O  S  A  Q  S  Q  Q
```

Name: _____ Date: _____

Step on It!

Underline the root *ped* or *pod* in the words below. Choose six words to write in the chart. Then tell what each word has to do with foot or feet.

pedal	pedestrian	centipede	podiatry
biped	backpedal	orthopedic	peddle
pedicure	pedometer	tripod	impede

Word	What does this word have to do with <u>feet</u>?

Name: _____ Date: _____

Breaking Through

Underline the root *rupt* in the words below.

erupt	bankrupt	interrupt	disrupt
rupture	abrupt	corrupt	

Unscramble the words. (Hint: Look at the words above.) **Copy the numbered letters in the boxes with the same number below. Then read the secret message!**

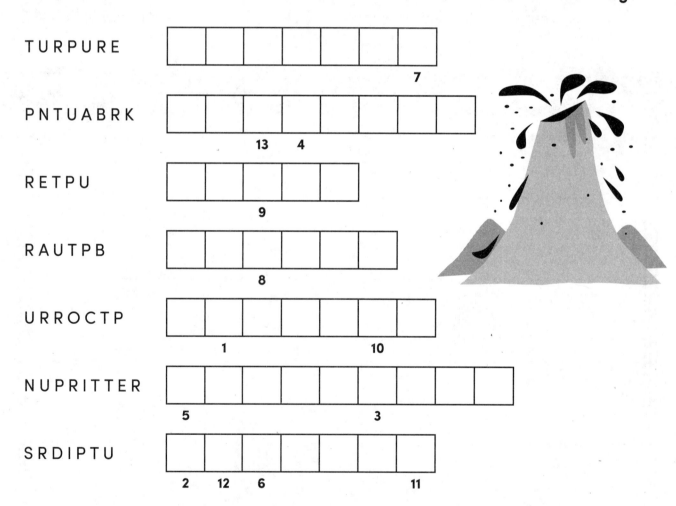

T U R P U R E

7

P N T U A B R K

13 4

R E T P U

9

R A U T P B

8

U R R O C T P

1   10

N U P R I T T E R

5   3

S R D I P T U

2 12 6   11

Secret Message:

G ___ ___ ___   W ___ ___ ___   ___ ___   ___ ___ ___ ___ ___ ___ ___G!
   1   1   2   1   3   4   5   6   7   8   9   10 11 12 13

Race the Roots

Number of Players: 2

Materials
- Race the Roots game board* (pages 62–63)
- A counter or marker for each player

*Photocopy the pages and glue them on the inside of a file folder.

How to Play

1. Each player takes a turn spinning the spinner to get a word root. At his turn, a player then moves his marker along the racetrack until he lands on a word with that root. To stay at that spot, the player has to read the word.

2. If a player lands on "Move 1" in the spinner, she moves her marker forward one space and reads the word in that space.

3. Play continues until both racers have reached the finish line. Then they can play again.

SPINNER

Use a pencil, pointed end at the middle of the spinner, and a paper clip to spin around the tip of the pencil.

Race the Roots

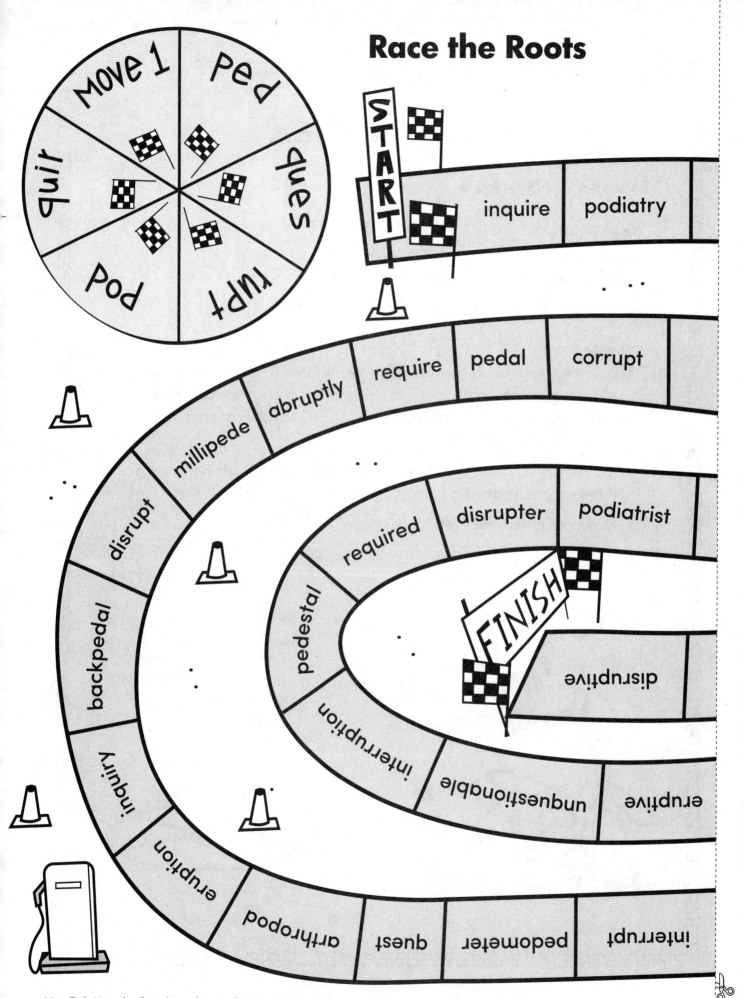

Move 1 · **ped** · **ques** · **rupt** · **pod** · **quir**

START · inquire · podiatry

require · pedal · corrupt

abruptly · millipede

disrupt

backpedal

inquiry

eruption · arthropod · quest · pedometer · interrupt

eruptive · unquestionable · interruption · pedestal · required · disrupter · podiatrist

disruptive

FINISH

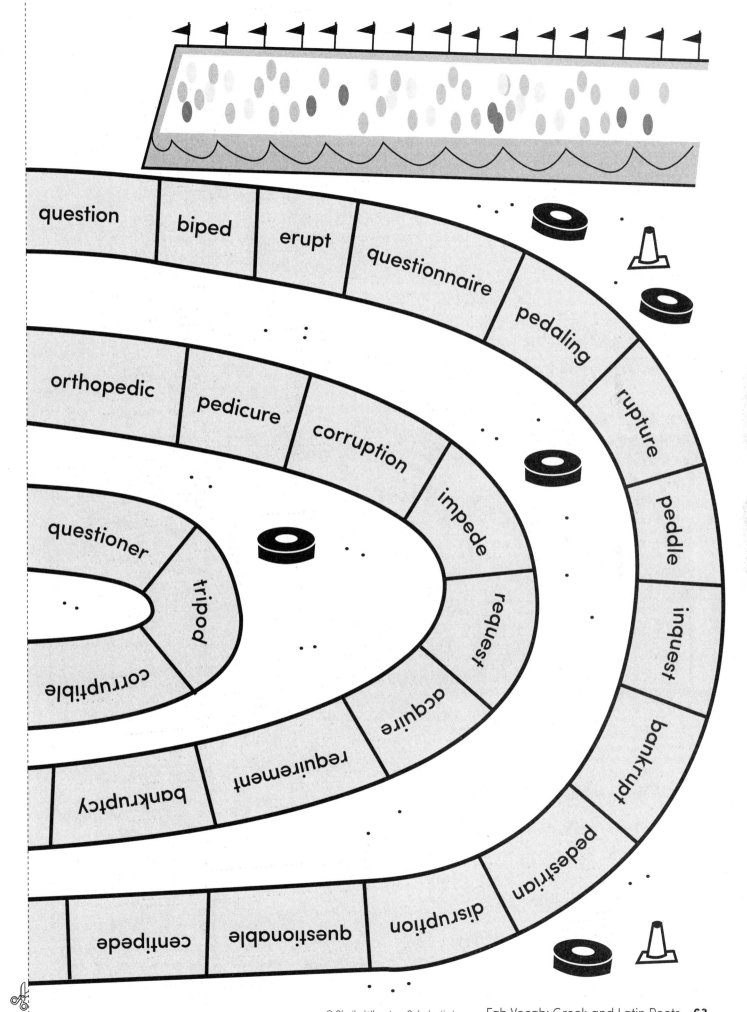

question

biped

erupt

questionnaire

pedaling

rupture

peddle

inquest

bankrupt

pedestrian

disruption

questionable

centipede

bankruptcy

requirement

acquire

request

impede

corruption

pedicure

orthopedic

questioner

tripod

corruptible

Fab Vocab: Greek and Latin Roots

SCRIB/SCRIPT

The roots *scrib* and *script* come from Latin. They mean "to write."

subscribe – to sign (<u>write</u>) one's name to a document; to receive a periodical (<u>written</u> words) on a regular basis

describe – to tell in <u>written</u> or spoken words

script – hand<u>writing</u>; something <u>written</u>

SPEC/SPECT

The roots *spec* and *spect* come from Latin. They mean "to see or look."

speculate – to <u>look</u> at and examine or wonder about a subject

spectator – a person who <u>looks</u> on or observes

spectacles – glasses (to <u>see</u> with); unusual or impressive public displays (to <u>look</u> at)

TAIN

The root *tain* comes from Latin. It means "to hold."

sustain – to support, keep going, or <u>hold</u> up

contain – to <u>hold</u> or have within

entertain – to amuse; to receive as a guest; to <u>hold</u> in mind

Name: _____ Date: _____

Let's Write!

In each box, write a word that uses the root *scrib* or *script*. Circle the root in each word. Then tell what the word means and draw a picture to illustrate it.

Name: _____ Date: _____

Looking for Words

Fill in the blanks with *spec* or *spect* to make real words.
Read each word and write it where it belongs in the puzzle.

Across

1. in _____

5. _____ ulate

7. pro _____

8. re _____

9. _____ ific

Down

2. _____ ator

3. _____ imen

4. intro _____ ive

5. _____ acle

6. a _____

Name: _____ Date: _____

Hold It!

Underline the root *tain* in the words below. Choose six words to write in the chart. Then tell what each word has to do with "to hold."

contain	container	maintain	sustain	entertain
obtain	abstain	attain	pertain	certain

Word	What does this word have to do with "to hold"?

Word Root Tic-Tac-Toe

Number of Players: 2

Materials
- Word Root Tic-Tac-Toe game board* (pages 69–73)
- Pencil or wipe-off marker

   *You can laminate the game boards or put them in page protectors for students to use with wipe-off markers.

How to Play

1. Players share a game board and take turns writing the roots *scrib*, *script*, *spec*, *spect*, or *tain* in the blanks to make real words. A player has to say the word aloud before he can write and claim the space.

2. The first player to get three spaces in a row vertically, horizontally, or diagonally wins that round.

> **NOTE**
> This game goes fast, so players should use the same game board a couple of times before getting a different one.

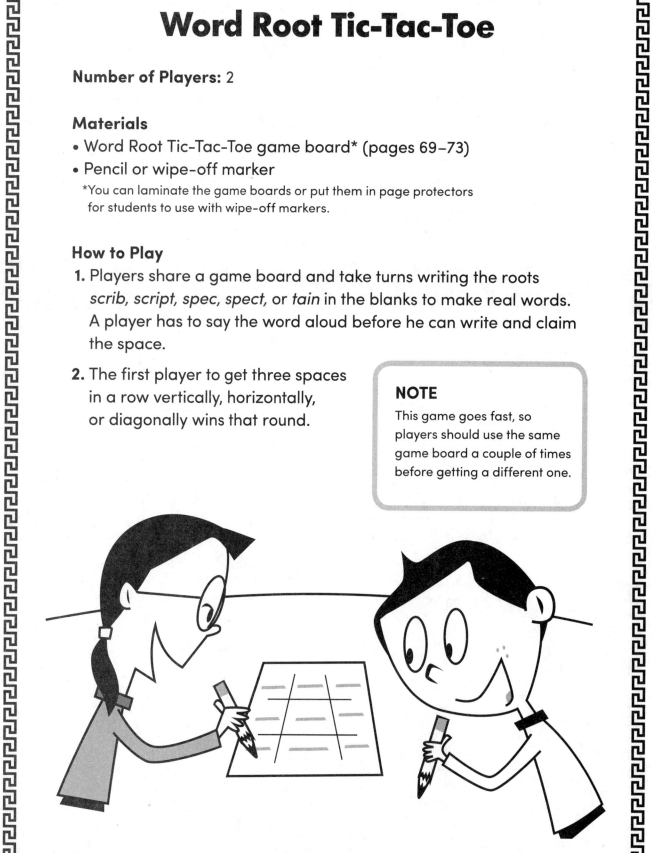

Word Root Tic-Tac-Toe 1

con_____	in_____e	re_____
_____ure	in_____	pro_____
de_____ion	main_____	cer_____ty

Word Root Tic-Tac-Toe 2

_____ator	cer_____ty	de_____e
_____imen	main_____	pre_____ion
re_____	manu_____	pro_____

Word Root Tic-Tac-Toe 3

_____ator	con_____	in_____e
_____ble	_____ure	_____tacle
at_____	de_____ion	ob_____

Word Root Tic-Tac-Toe 4

re_____able	_____tator	pre_____ion
_____tacle	sus_____	sub_____ion
_____ulate	abs_____	con_____er

Word Root Tic-Tac-Toe 5

in_____	_____ulate	pro_____
pre_____ion	per_____	sub_____ion
abs_____	_____ure	_____ific

Word Root Review

By teaching students to recognize Greek and Latin roots, you have opened up a whole new world for them! They now have a better vocabulary and a handy tool for attacking new words. Hopefully they have already begun to notice roots in their readings.

This section features a Word Root Hunt, five games, and eight reproducible practice pages for students to review the word roots they have learned. Bring out these activities at any time to reinforce the learning that has taken place and to check for students' understanding.

Directions for Word Root Hunt

Help students make real-world connections by challenging them to go on a Word Root Hunt. Have them search for the roots they know in books, posters, notes, billboards, ads, and so on. Distribute copies of the Word Root Hunt recording page (page 75) and have students list the words they find. Be sure to take a few minutes afterwards for students to share some of their findings.

Name: _____   Date: _____

Word Root Hunt

geo	dem	form	logy	graph

meter	lit	micro	gress	ques	ject

quir	phobia	ped	pod	script	phon

tele	photo	grad	scrib	duc

chron	bio	flect	duct

rupt	tain	spec	spect	flex

Write the words you discover in the space below. Circle the roots.

_____	_____
_____	_____
_____	_____
_____	_____
_____	_____
_____	_____
_____	_____

Word Root Memory

Number of Players: 2

Materials
• Word Root Memory cards (pages 77–78)

How to Play

1. Shuffle the cards and arrange them facedown in rows.

2. Players take turns turning over two cards, keeping them in their spots. At his turn, a player tries to match a root (cards in bold print) to the rest of the word (cards with a blank). For example, *bio* and _____*sphere* are a match because they make the word *biosphere*.

3. If a player finds a match, she reads aloud the word. If her partner agrees that it is a real word, the player keeps both cards and gets another turn. If it's not a real word, the other player takes a turn.

4. Play continues until all cards have been matched up. The person with the most cards wins.

5. Players can shuffle the cards again to play another round.

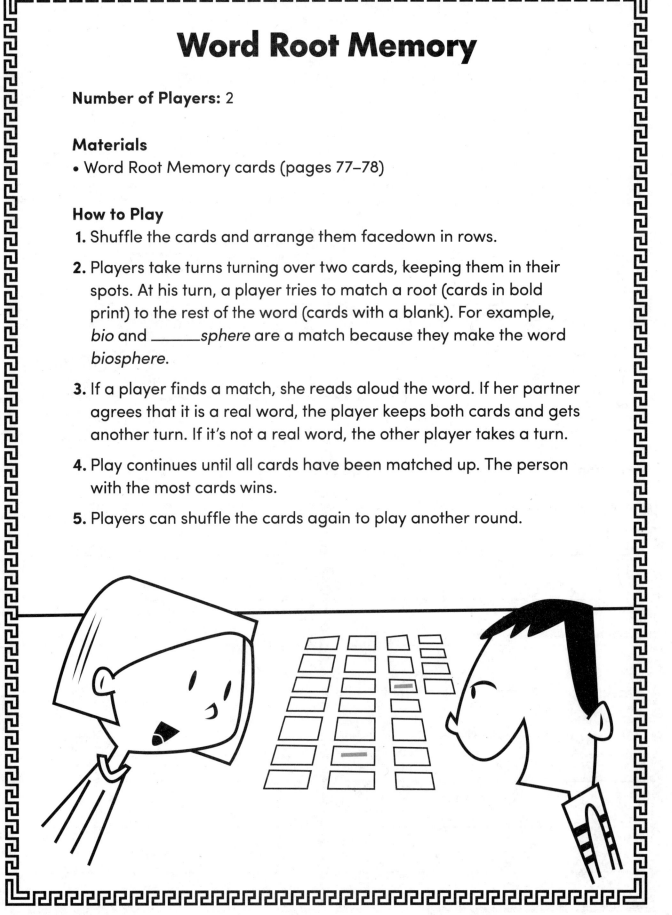

Word Root Memory Cards

_____ sphere	tele _____ e	ob _____ ion
manu _____	_____ icle	_____ ocracy
_____ metry	photo _____	centi _____
_____ wave	arachno _____	_____ vision
con _____ or	uni _____	_____ uate
main _____	_____ tion	_____ ulate

Word Root Memory Cards

bio	phon	ject
script	chron	dem
geo	graph	meter
micro	phobia	tele
duct	form	grad
tain	ques	spec

Word Root Bingo

Number of Players: 2 to 6, plus a Caller

Materials
- Word Root Bingo game boards (pages 80–85)
- Word Root cards (page 86)
- small brown paper bag
- markers (pennies, buttons, and so on)

How to Play

1. Mix up the Word Root cards and put them in the paper bag or in a pile. Players put a marker on the FREE space on their bingo game boards.

2. The Caller pulls out a card, shows it to the players, then reads aloud the word root on the card.

3. Players try to find a word on their game board that contains that root. Many times there will be more than one matching word on the game board. A player must choose one word and leave his marker on that space for the rest of the round, not switching it to another word.

4. Play continues until a player has covered five words in a line across, down, or diagonally. That player yells out "Bingo" and reads back the covered words to check them with the roots that have been called.

5. Players clear their boards while the Caller returns the used Word Root cards in the bag for another round.

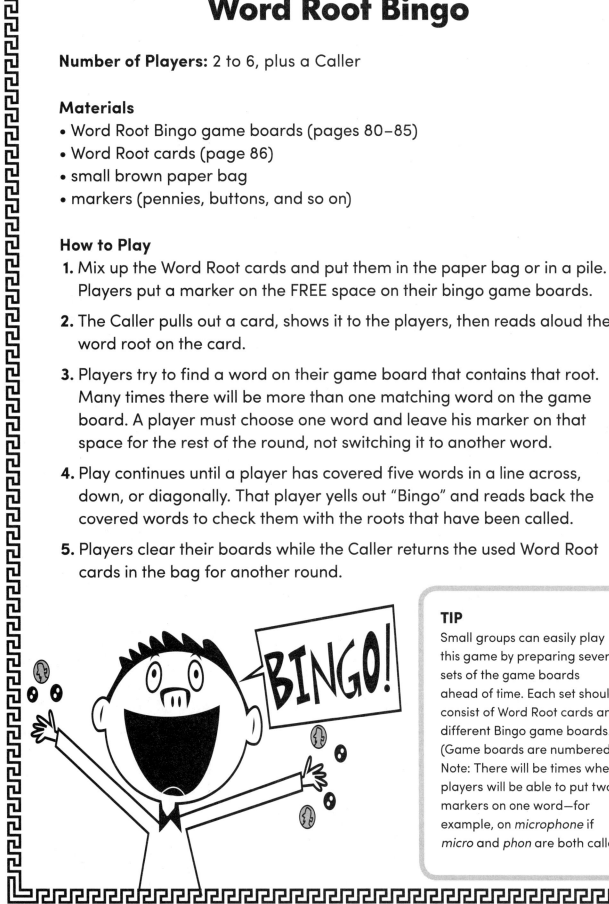

TIP

Small groups can easily play this game by preparing several sets of the game boards ahead of time. Each set should consist of Word Root cards and different Bingo game boards. (Game boards are numbered.) Note: There will be times when players will be able to put two markers on one word—for example, on *microphone* if *micro* and *phon* are both called.

Word Root Bingo Game Board 1

photograph	synchronize	container	biography	microphone
technology	literature	flexible	democratic	centipede
formation	spectator	**FREE**	microscope	produce
question	diameter	phobia	telegram	paragraph
interject	interrupt	graduation	geothermal	description

Word Root Bingo Game Board 2

spectator	question	produce	interject	paragraph
container	literature	flexible	biography	technology
description	microphone	FREE	synchronize	diameter
interrupt	photograph	formation	democratic	microscope
centipede	telegram	graduation	geothermal	phobia

Word Root Bingo Game Board 3

description	biography	geothermal	literature	synchronize
phobia	flexible	telegram	paragraph	interject
question	technology	**FREE**	interrupt	microscope
democratic	container	diameter	graduation	spectator
microphone	produce	centipede	formation	photograph

Word Root Bingo Game Board 4

literature	graduation	geothermal	interrupt	synchronize
paragraph	description	produce	photograph	spectator
technology	microphone	**FREE**	microscope	interject
container	phobia	formation	centipede	democratic
biography	telegram	question	diameter	flexible

Word Root Bingo Game Board 5

centipede	democratic	flexible	phobia	spectator
diameter	photograph	question	formation	microscope
biography	interject	**FREE**	microphone	geothermal
container	telegram	description	synchronize	interrupt
paragraph	literature	technology	produce	graduation

Word Root Bingo Game Board 6

formation	interrupt	geothermal	synchronize	question
container	microscope	telegram	photograph	biography
diameter	spectator	FREE	paragraph	flexible
produce	graduation	technology	democratic	literature
centipede	phobia	microphone	description	interject

Word Root Cards

bio	geo	meter
chron	graph	micro
dem	logy	phobia
rupt	ped/pod	ques/quir

phon	duc/duct	grad/gress
photo	flex/flect	ject
tele	form	lit
scrib/script	spec/spect	tain

Word Root Checkers

Number of Players: 2

Materials
- Word Root Checkers game board* (pages 88–89)
- 24 checker pieces or 2 different colors of counters (12 counters for each player)

*Photocopy the pages and glue them to the inside of a file folder.

How to Play

1. Before beginning the game, partners should read all of the words on the game board together. They can then decide what color of squares to play on—white or gray.

2. Players place their counters on that color on their side of the board. Then they play a regular checkers game. The only difference is that before a player can stay on a spot, she must read aloud the word on that space. You might want to have players identify the root, too.

3. After they finish the game, encourage players to play on the other color of squares.

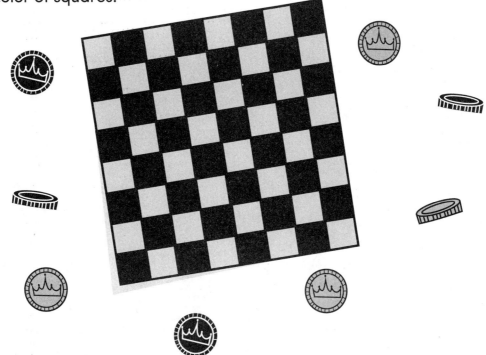

deflect	chronic	aggressive	inscription
paragraph	education	gradual	trajectory
maintain	reduce	transform	barometer
specific	orthopedic	geography	biosphere
acrophobia	request	synchronize	literary
container	diameter	telecast	grade
flexor	arthropod	micron	saxophone
flexible	telepathy	interrupt	abduct

Glue the other side of the game board on this strip.

reflection	bankrupt	technology	eruption
photogenic	microphone	question	phobia
pedicure	telephone	epidemic	spectator
literature	inquire	prescription	biography
centipede	specimen	scribble	inquiry
zoology	inspection	graphic	progress
photograph	geode	introduction	tripod
demagogue	perform	inscribe	objection

KABOOM!

Number of Players: whole class, plus a Caller

Materials
- KABOOM! game board for each student (page 91)
- KABOOM! Word Root cards (pages 92–93)
- small brown paper bag
- black marker for each student
- light-colored crayon for each student
  (yellow, pink, orange, light green, light blue, etc.)

How to Play
1. Have students use a black marker to fill in the spaces of their game board with words containing the roots listed on the top of the board. They should write one word in each space. Encourage them to use as many different roots as possible.

2. Place the Word Root cards in a paper bag. To play the game, the Caller picks a card from the bag and reads it aloud. Anyone who has a word with that root on his or her game board should read the word and color in that space. Take a minute to have students share their words with the class or with others close by.

3. If the Caller draws out a card that says **KABOOM!** all students get up and move to another game board, taking their crayon with them.

4. When the Caller reads a new root, students color the word with that root on the new game board in front of them. Continue playing until one game board is completely filled.

KABOOM! Game Board

WORD ROOTS

bio	chron	dem	geo	tain
graph	logy	meter	micro	spec/spect
phobia	phon	photo	tele	scrib/script
duc/duct	flex/flect	form	grad/gress	rupt
ject	lit	ques/quir	ped/pod	

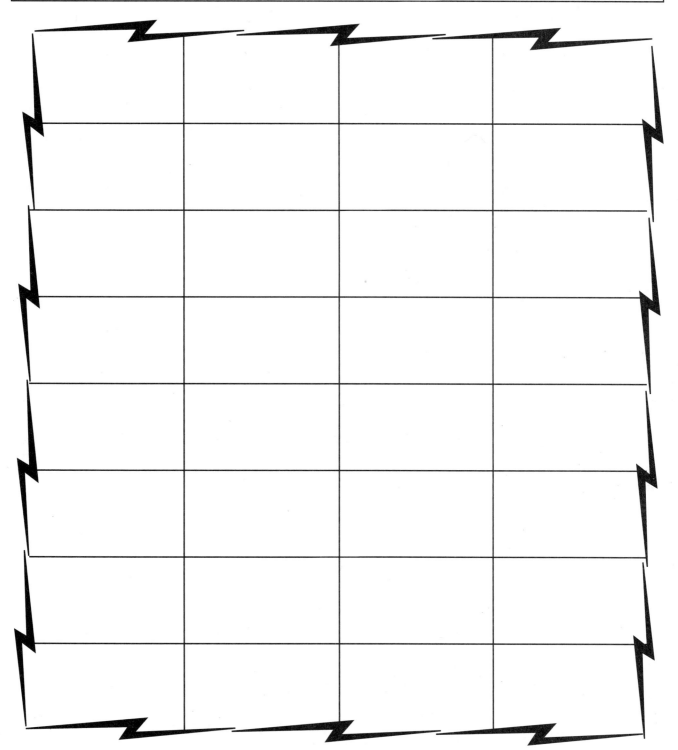

KABOOM! Word Root Cards

bio	chron	dem
geo	graph	logy
meter	micro	phobia
phon	photo	tele
duc	duct	flex
flect	form	grad
gress	ject	lit

KABOOM! Word Root Cards

ques	quir	ped
pod	rupt	scrib
script	spec	spect
tain	*KABOOM!*	*KABOOM!*
KABOOM!	*KABOOM!*	*KABOOM!*
KABOOM!	*KABOOM!*	*KABOOM!*
KABOOM!	*KABOOM!*	*KABOOM!*

Root Read-a-Row

Number of Players: 2 to 4

Materials
- Root Read-a-Row game board for each player (pages 95–100)
- Read-a-Row Word Root cards (page 101)
- small brown paper bag

How to Play

1. Mix up the Word Root cards and put them in the paper bag.

2. Players take turns reaching into the bag to get a card. At her turn, a player reads the root and decides if it can be used to complete a word on her game board. (Depending on students' abilities, you might want to have the whole group help figure out whether or not the player can use the root.) Once a Word Root card is placed on the game board to complete a word, it may not be moved from that space until the round is over.

3. Players continue taking turns in this way. If a player gets a card he doesn't need, he returns it in the bag, and the next player takes a turn.

4. Play continues until someone gets five words in a row vertically, horizontally, or diagonally. (The middle square is a free space.)

5. To begin a new round, return all the word cards in the bag. Players may trade or choose a different game board.

Root Read-a-Row 1

ob _____	de _____	_____ ic	_____ synthesis	_____ graphy
re _____	syn _____ ize	con _____	_____ ocrat	per _____
tri _____	_____ graph	**FREE**	_____ logy	main _____
e _____	dis _____	audio _____	_____ logist	pro _____
back _____ al	speedo _____	_____ in	_____ vision	_____ erature

Root Read-a-Row 2

sus ————	———— in ————	———— copy	sub ———— e	kilo ————
in ————	———— eracy	———— graphy	———— ible	———— tion
de ————	———— logy	**FREE**	claustro ————	uni ————
———— wave	———— e	up ———— e	re ————	auto ————
———— estrian	———— ocratic	tele ———— e	centi ————	———— gram

Root Read-a-Row 3

re ___	dis ___	per ___	___ graphy	___ ic
land ___	audio ___	arachno ___	sus ___	milli ___ e
___ eracy	pro ___	**FREE**	___ surgery	ob ___
___ ocratic	___ e	tri ___	___ logy	___ logist
con ___	uni ___	___ in	para ___	___ graph

___ graphy	pro ___	___ surgery	back ___ al	___ vision
___ ic	___ e	re ___	para ___	ag ___ ive
arachno ___	___ graph	**FREE**	per ___	ob ___
dis ___	___ logy	syn ___ ize	in ___ e	de ___
___ in	___ eral	pre ___	thermo ___	con ___

Root Read-a-Row 5

manu ___	ab ___	zoo ___	im ___ e	___ ocracy
speedo ___	tele ___	de ___	acro ___	ear ___ e
___ logy	in ___ y	**FREE**	main ___	pro ___
in ___	audio ___	___ phone	dia ___	land ___
pro ___	il ___ erate	___ graphy	re ___	cor ___

Root Read-a-Row 6

inter ___	de ___	___ erature	photo ___	pro ___
___ ual	zoo ___	___ logist	de ___ e	hydro ___
re ___	ortho ___ ic	**FREE**	___ ocrat	___ synthesis
___ logy	in ___	___ al	mega ___ e	___ acle
con ___	ob ___	ac ___ e	___ graphy	___ scope

Read-a-Row Word Root Cards

bio	chron	dem	geo	graph	logy	meter	micro	phobia	
photo	tele	duct	flex	flect	form	grad	gress	ject	
ques	quir	ped	pod	rupt	scrib	script	spec	spect	
bio	chron	dem	geo	graph	logy	meter	micro	phobia	
photo	tele	duct	flex	flect	form	grad	gress	ject	
ques	quir	ped	pod	rupt	scrib	script	spec	spect	
bio	chron	dem	geo	graph	logy	meter	micro	phobia	
photo	tele	duct	flex	flect	form	grad	gress	ject	
ques	quir	ped	pod	rupt	scrib	script	spec	spect	
phon	lit	tain	phon	lit	tain	phon	lit	tain	

Name: _____   Date: _____

Getting to the Root of Words

Choose six words from the box below and write them in the first column of the chart. Underline each root and write its meaning. Then write the definition of the whole word.

| uniform | democracy | geography | microscope | earphone |
| progress | autograph | conductor | inquire | literate |

Word	What does the <u>root</u> mean?	What does the <u>whole word</u> mean?

Name: _____   Date: _____

Putting Down Roots

Choose six words from the box below and write them in the first column of the chart. Underline each root and write its meaning. Then write the definition of the whole word.

| mythology | phobia | erupt | telephoto | reflect |
| speedometer | photosynthesis | eject | pedestrian | spectator |

Word	What does the <u>root</u> mean?	What does the <u>whole word</u> mean?

Name: _____ Date: _____

Taking Root

| rupt | graph | meter | photo | ped | tain |

Read each root above and think about its meaning. Then choose a root to fill in each blank to make a word. Write a sentence using the word you made.

1. _____ copy

_____

_____

2. para _____

_____

_____

3. _____ al

_____

_____

4. dia _____

_____

_____

5. sus _____

_____

_____

Name: _____ Date: _____

Write a Root

| scrib | ques | spect | lit | logy | gress |

Read each root above and think about its meaning. Then choose a root to fill in each blank to make a word. Write a sentence using the word you made.

1. in _____

_____

_____

2. _____ tion

_____

_____

3. _____ erature

_____

_____

4. pro _____

_____

_____

5. _____ ble

_____

_____

Name: _____ Date: _____

Growing Words

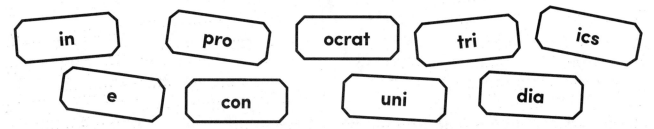

in pro ocrat tri ics

e con uni dia

How many words can you make by adding the above letters to these roots?

ROOTS	WORDS I CAN MAKE
PHON	
METER	
POD	
DEM	
LOGY	
SPECT	
GRAD	
DUCT	
FORM	
TAIN	

Name: _____ Date: _____

Rooting for Words

pro | graphy | scope | inter | sphere

dis | gram | ic | re

How many words can you make by adding the above letters to these roots?

ROOTS	WORDS I CAN MAKE
GEO	
CHRON	
BIO	
GRAPH	
JECT	
TELE	
FLEX	
PHOTO	
RUPT	
MICRO	

Name: _____ Date: _____

Looking for the Right Word

Read the words in the box and underline the roots. Think about what each root means as you read the sentences, looking for clues to help you. Then fill in the blanks with the correct words.

paragraph	deflect	uniform	microscope
diameter	centipede	inscription	introduce

1. The _____ on the necklace read, "Love from Mom and Dad."

2. She wrote a _____ about her dog.

3. The crawling _____ had many feet.

4. During math, we measured the _____ of a circle.

5. Will you please _____ me to your friend?

6. The knight used his shield to _____ the arrows.

7. In science class we used a _____ to look at parts of a leaf.

8. The baseball player got his _____ dirty when he slid to home plate.

Name: _____ Date: _____

The Final Word

Read the words in the box and underline the roots. Think about what each root means as you read the sentences, looking for clues to help you. Then fill in the blanks with the correct words.

epidemic	chronological	biology	graphic
arachnophobia	microphone	literature	photographer

1. He loves _____ novels because he enjoys looking at pictures.

2. It was hard to hear the speaker because the _____ stopped working.

3. I like learning about living things in my _____ class.

4. Don't let him see that spider. He has _____!

5. I love to read good _____.

6. Read the story then tell what happened in _____ order.

7. Many people got sick during the _____ last year.

8. The _____ had to be very quiet to get good pictures of the birds.

Answer Key

page 17
Answers will vary.

page 18
1. c   5. b
2. g   6. a
3. f   7. e
4. d
Sentences will vary.

page 19
What does the root *dem* mean?
People
1. epidemic
2. democracy
3. demographics
4. Democratic
5. demagogue

page 23
Answers will vary.

page 24
1. photograph   5. seismograph
2. autograph   6. paragraph
3. polygraph   7. telegraph
4. calligraphy   8. graph
Biography; sentences will vary.

page 25
1. myths
2. ecosystems
3. life, living matter
4. animals
5. time of events
6. music
7. hearing
8. rocks, earth
9. crime, criminals
Answers will vary.

page 30
What does the root *meter* mean?
Measure
1. audiometer
2. pedometer
3. kilometer
4. barometer
5. speedometer
6. centimeter
7. diameter
8. meter

page 31
Answers will vary.

page 32

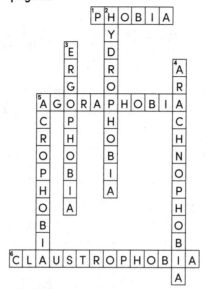

page 38
1. megaphone   5. telephone
2. headphones   6. microphone
3. saxophone   7. xylophone
4. phonics   8. earphone
Sentences will vary.

page 39
Answers will vary.

page 40
Answers will vary.

page 44

page 45
1. reflection   4. flex
2. flexible   5. reflex
3. deflect   6. reflector

page 46
What does the root word *form*
mean? Shape
Answers will vary.

page 51
1. d   5. b
2. a   6. c
3. h   7. f
4. g   8. e
Sentences will vary.

page 52

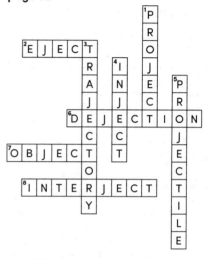

page 53
Answers will vary.

page 58

page 59
Answers will vary.

page 60
RUPTURE; BANKRUPT; ERUPT;
ABRUPT; CORRUPT; INTERRUPT;
DISRUPT
Secret message: GOOD WORK IS
ERUPTING!

page 65
Answers will vary.

page 66

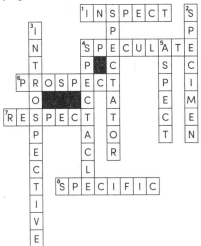

page 67

Answers will vary.

page 69

contain	inscribe	respect, retain
scripture	inspect	prospect
description	maintain	certainty

page 70

spectator	certainty	describe
specimen	maintain	prescription
respect, retain, rescript	manuscript	prospect

page 71

spectator	contain, conscript	inscribe
scribble	scripture	spectacle
attain	description	obtain

page 72

respectable	spectator	prescription
spectacle	sustain, suspect	subscription
speculate	abstain	container

page 73

inspect	speculate	prospect
prescription	pertain	subscription
abstain	scripture	specific

page 75

Answers will vary.

page 77

biosphere, telephone, objection, manuscript, chronicle, democracy, geometry, photograph, centimeter, microwave, arachnophobia, television, conductor, uniform, graduate, maintain, question, speculate

page 95

Row 1: object, obtain; deduct, deflect, deform, detain, deject; chronic, graphic, phonic; photosynthesis; biography, geography, photography, telegraphy

Row 2: retain, respect, rescript, reject, regress, reform, reflect, reflex; synchronize; contain, conduct, conform, congress, conscript; democrat; perform, pertain

Row 3: trilogy, tripod; micrograph, photograph, telegraph; FREE SPACE; biology, geology; maintain

Row 4: eject, egress, erupt; disrupt; audiology, audiometer; biologist, geologist; prospect, product, progress, project

Row 5: backpedal; speedometer; inspect, induct, inflect, inform, ingress, inject; television; literature

page 96

Row 1: sustain; inspect, induct, inflect, inform, ingress, inject; deduct, deflect, deform, detain, deject; microwave; pedestrian

Row 2: inspection, induction, injection, inflection, inscription; literacy; biology, geology; eject, egress, erupt; democratic

Row 3: photocopy; biography, geography, photography, telegraphy; FREE SPACE; upgrade; telephone

Row 4: subscribe; flexible; claustrophobia; retain, respect, rescript, reject, regress, reform, reflect; centimeter

Row 5: kilometer; question; uniform; autograph, autophobia; microgram, photogram, telegram

page 97

Row 1: retain, respect, rescript, reject, regress, reform, reflect; disrupt; perform, pertain; biology, geology; chronic, graphic, phonic

Row 2: biography, geography, photography, telegraphy; audiology, audiometer; arachnophobia; sustain; millipede

Row 3: literacy; prospect, product, progress, project; FREE SPACE; microsurgery; object, obtain

Row 4: landform; democratic; eject, egress, erupt; trilogy, tripod; biologist, geologist

Row 5: contain, conduct, conform, congress, conscript; uniform; inspect, induct, inflect, inform, ingress, inject; paragraph, parameter; micrograph, photograph, telegraph

page 98

Row 1: television; aggressive; object, obtain; deduct, deflect, deform, detain, deject; contain, conduct, conform, congress, conscript

Row 2: backpedal; paragraph, parameter; perform, pertain; inquire, inscribe; thermometer, thermograph, thermoform

Row 3: microsurgery; retain, respect, rescript, reject, regress, reform, reflect; FREE SPACE; synchronize; preform, prescript

Row 4: prospect, product, progress, project; eject, egress, erupt; micrograph, photograph, telegraph; biology, geology; literal

Row 5: biography, geography, photography, telegraphy; chronic, graphic, phonic; arachnophobia; disrupt; inspect, induct, inflect, inform, ingress, inject

page 99
Row 1: manuscript; abduct, abject, abrupt; zoology, zoophobia; impede; democracy

Row 2: speedometer; telegraph, telemeter; deduct, deflect, deform, detain, deject; acrophobia; earphone

Row 3: biology, geology; inquiry; FREE SPACE; maintain; prospect, product, progress, project

Row 4: inspect, induct, inflect, inform, ingress, inject; audiology, audiometer; telephone, microphone; diameter, diagraph; landform

Row 5: prospect, product, progress, project; illiterate; biography, geography, telegraphy, photography; retain, respect, rescript, reject, regress, reform, reflect; corrupt

page 100
Row 1: interrupt, interject; gradual; retain, respect, rescript, reject, regress, reform, reflect; biology, geology; contain, conduct, conform, congress, conscript

Row 2: deduct, deflect, deform, detain, deject; zoology, zoophobia; orthopedic, orthographic; inspect, induct, inflect, inform, ingress, inject; object, obtain

Row 3: literature; biologist, geologist; FREE SPACE; formal, pedal; acquire

Row 4: photograph, photometer, photophobia; degrade; democrat; megaphone; biography, geography, telegraphy, photography

Row 5: prospect, product, progress, project; hydrograph, hydrology, hydrometer, hydrophobia; photosynthesis, biosynthesis; spectacle; microscope, telescope

page 102

Word	What does the root word mean?	What does the whole word mean?
uni**form**	form – shape	same shape
democracy	dem – people	government by the people
geography	geo – earth	science that deals with the earth
microscope	micro – small	tool to view small objects
ear**phon**e	phon – sound	tool to hear sounds that goes in ear
pro**gress**	gress – step	moving forward by steps
auto**graph**	graph – to write	one's written signature
con**duct**or	duct – to lead	someone who leads a group
in**quir**e	quir – to ask	to ask a question
literate	lit – letters	able to read letters

page 103

Word	What does the root word mean?	What does the whole word mean?
mytho**logy**	logy – study of	study of myths
phobia	phobia – fear	fear
e**rupt**	rupt – break	to break through a surface
telephoto	tele – far	lens to see an image from far away
re**flect**	flect – bend or curve	light bends so you can see image
speedo**meter**	meter – to measure	tool that measures speed
photosynthesis	photo – light	process that uses light to make food for plants
e**ject**	ject – throw	to throw out
pedestrian	ped – foot	walker going on foot
spectator	spect – to see or look	someone who looks on

page 104
1. photocopy; sentences will vary.
2. paragraph or parameter; sentences will vary.
3. pedal; sentences will vary.
4. diameter or diagraph; sentences will vary.
5. sustain; sentences will vary.

page 105
1. inspect or ingress; sentences will vary.
2. question; sentences will vary.
3. literature; sentences will vary.
4. progress or prospect; sentences will vary.
5. scribble; sentences will vary.

page 106
phon: phone, phonics
meter: diameter
pod: tripod
dem: democrat
logy: trilogy
spect: inspect, prospect
grad: grade
duct: product, conduct, induct
form: uniform, conform, inform
tain: contain

page 107
geo: geography, geosphere
chron: chronic
bio: biography, biosphere
graph: graphic, regraph
ject: interject, project, reject
tele: telescope, telegram
flex: reflex
photo: photography
rupt: disrupt, interrupt
micro: microscope

page 108
1. inscription
2. paragraph
3. centipede
4. diameter
5. introduce
6. deflect
7. microscope
8. uniform

page 109
1. graphic
2. microphone
3. biology
4. arachnophobia
5. literature
6. chronological
7. epidemic
8. photographer